Garfield

With Love From Me To You

JIM DAVIS

RAVETTE BOOKS

First published by
Ravette Books Limited 1992
Reprinted 1992 (twice)

Printed and bound in Great Britain
for Ravette Books Limited,
8 Clifford Street, London W1X 1RB
An Egmont Company
by Cox & Wyman Ltd, Reading

ISBN 1 85304 392 3

CHECKING FOR A PULSE

I HATE THAT

SCHLUP.

OH, JON

JiM DAViS 9-4

© 1990 United Feature Syndicate, Inc.

© 1990 United Feature Syndicate, Inc.

JIM DAVIS 10-10

© 1990 United Feature Syndicate, Inc.

JIM DAVIS 10-12

POOMP!

IS IT JUST ME? OR IS EVERYBODY IN A BAD MOOD TODAY?

JIM DAVIS 10-15

I'M MORE BORED THAN YOU ARE

ARE NOT!

JIM DAVIS 10-19

© 1990 United Feature Syndicate, Inc.

ALL RIGHT! I DO BELIEVE YOU HAVE HIT BOTTOM!

JiM DAViS 10-25

© 1990 United Feature Syndicate, Inc.

JIM DAVIS 11-1

© 1990 United Feature Syndicate, Inc.

JiM DAViS 11-12

© 1990 United Feature Syndicate, Inc.

© 1990 United Feature Syndicate, Inc.

© 1990 United Feature Syndicate, inc.

JIM DAVIS 12-10

SMACK!

STOP

© 1990 United Feature Syndicate, Inc.

© 1990 United Feature Syndicate, Inc.

JIM DAVIS 12-24

© 1990 United Feature Syndicate, Inc.

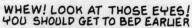

© 1990 United Feature Syndicate, Inc.

OTHER GARFIELD BOOKS IN THIS SERIES

COLOUR TV SPECIALS

Here Comes Garfield	£2.95
Garfield On The Town	£2.95
Garfield In The Rough	£2.95
Garfield In Disguise	£2.95
Garfield In Paradise	£2.95
Garfield Goes To Hollywood	£2.95
A Garfield Christmas	£2.95
Garfield's Thanksgiving	£2.95
Garfield's Feline Fantasies	£2.95
Garfield Gets A Life	£2.95
Garfield's Night Before Christmas	£3.95
Garfield's Tales Of Mystery	£3.95
Garfield's Scary Tales	£3.95
Garfield The Easter Bunny?	£3.95
Garfield Best Ever	£4.95
Garfield Selection	£5.95
Garfield His 9 Lives	£5.95
Garfield Diet Book	£4.95
Garfield Exercise Book	£4.95
Garfield Book Of Love	£5.95

All these books are available at your local bookshop or newsagent, or can be ordered direct from the publisher. Just tick the titles you require and fill in the form below. Prices and availability subject to change without notice.

Ravette Books, PO Box 11, Falmouth, Cornwall, TR10 9EN.

Please send a cheque or postal order for the value of the book, and add the following for postage and packing:
UK including BFPO – £1.00 per order.
OVERSEAS, including EIRE – £2.00 per order.
OR Please debit this amount from my Access/Visa Card (delete as appropriate).

Card Number ☐☐☐☐☐☐☐☐☐☐☐☐☐☐☐☐☐☐

AMOUNT £ ....   EXPIRY DATE ....

SIGNED ....

NAME ....

ADDRESS ....

....